SO-AEE-296

REAL BUGS
IN DISGUISE
IN 3-D

Advance PUBLISHERS   **DeAGOSTINI** COLLECT & DISCOVER

Copyright © 2010 Deagostini UK Ltd. All rights reserved

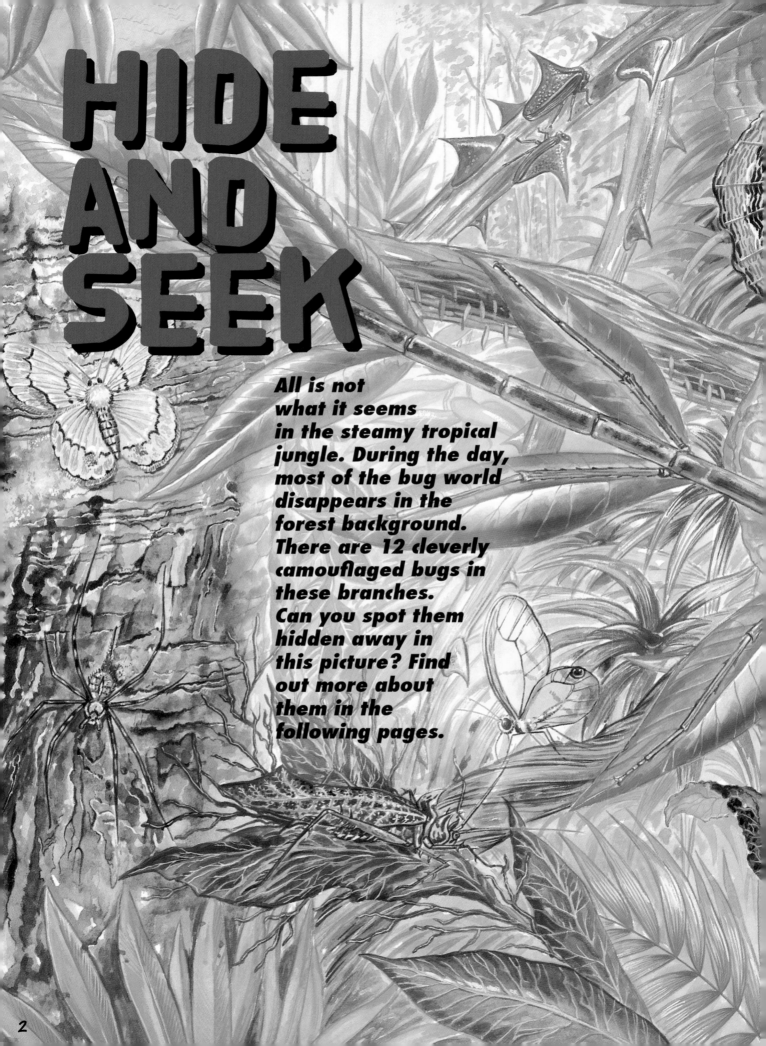

HIDE AND SEEK

All is not what it seems in the steamy tropical jungle. During the day, most of the bug world disappears in the forest background. There are 12 cleverly camouflaged bugs in these branches. Can you spot them hidden away in this picture? Find out more about them in the following pages.

HIDE AND SEEK

Did you spot all the bugs? To make it easier, we have cleared away the tangle of jungle. Read on to discover exactly how bugs do their disappearing acts.

Peruvian thorn bugs belong to the treehopper family. In the jungle they look just like thorns on a branch.

This moth called a geometrid is colored just like the tree trunk it is sitting on. It even has brown markings that look like bark.

Waiting on the lichen-covered bark, a lichen-colored spider is hoping to fool an insect into walking within its deadly reach.

Rain forest trees are usually covered with a thick layer of lichens. This lichenlike katydid has developed a camouflage to match the tangle of lichens.

See-through things are hard to spot in the dappled light of the forest. This clear-winged butterfly is well hidden, even when it is flying.

COLORFUL CAMOUFLAGE

Camouflage (say KA-meh-flazsh) is a disguise that helps a creature blend into its surroundings so that it can hide from both prey and predators.

DEVIOUS DISGUISES

Some bugs are the same color as the plants they live on. Bugs that rest in the open, such as moths, have patterns on their wings that break up their outline. Other bugs, such as stick insects, imitate the color and texture of the plants they live on.

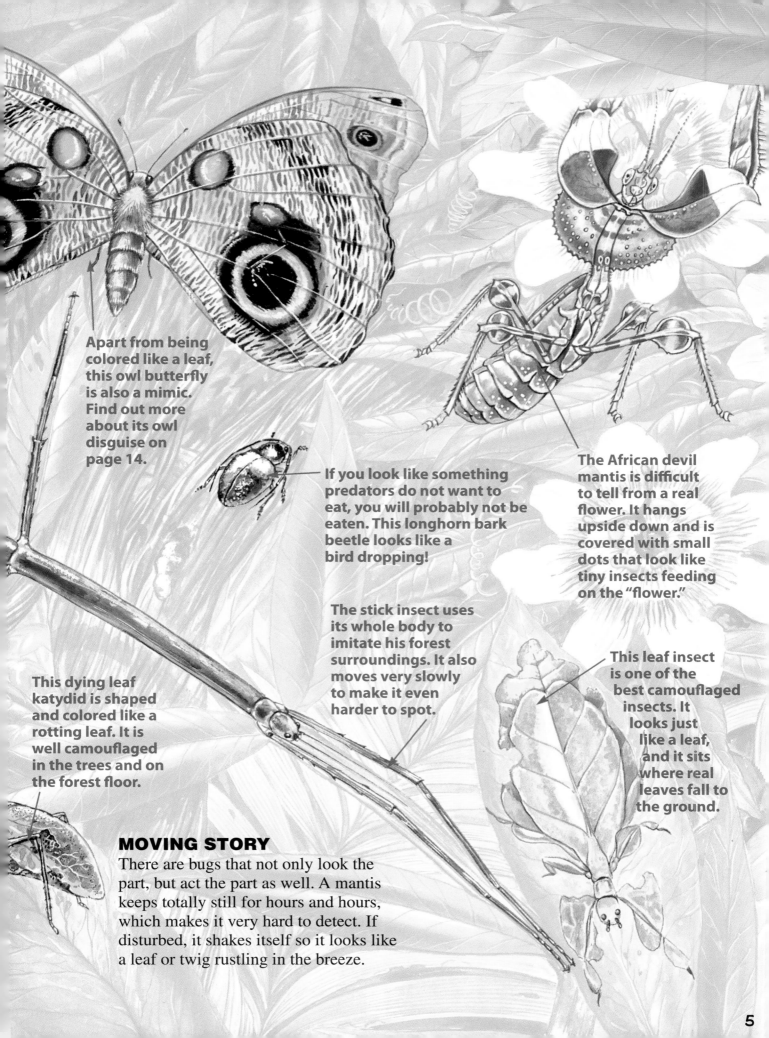

Apart from being colored like a leaf, this owl butterfly is also a mimic. Find out more about its owl disguise on page 14.

If you look like something predators do not want to eat, you will probably not be eaten. This longhorn bark beetle looks like a bird dropping!

The African devil mantis is difficult to tell from a real flower. It hangs upside down and is covered with small dots that look like tiny insects feeding on the "flower."

The stick insect uses its whole body to imitate his forest surroundings. It also moves very slowly to make it even harder to spot.

This dying leaf katydid is shaped and colored like a rotting leaf. It is well camouflaged in the trees and on the forest floor.

This leaf insect is one of the best camouflaged insects. It looks just like a leaf, and it sits where real leaves fall to the ground.

MOVING STORY

There are bugs that not only look the part, but act the part as well. A mantis keeps totally still for hours and hours, which makes it very hard to detect. If disturbed, it shakes itself so it looks like a leaf or twig rustling in the breeze.

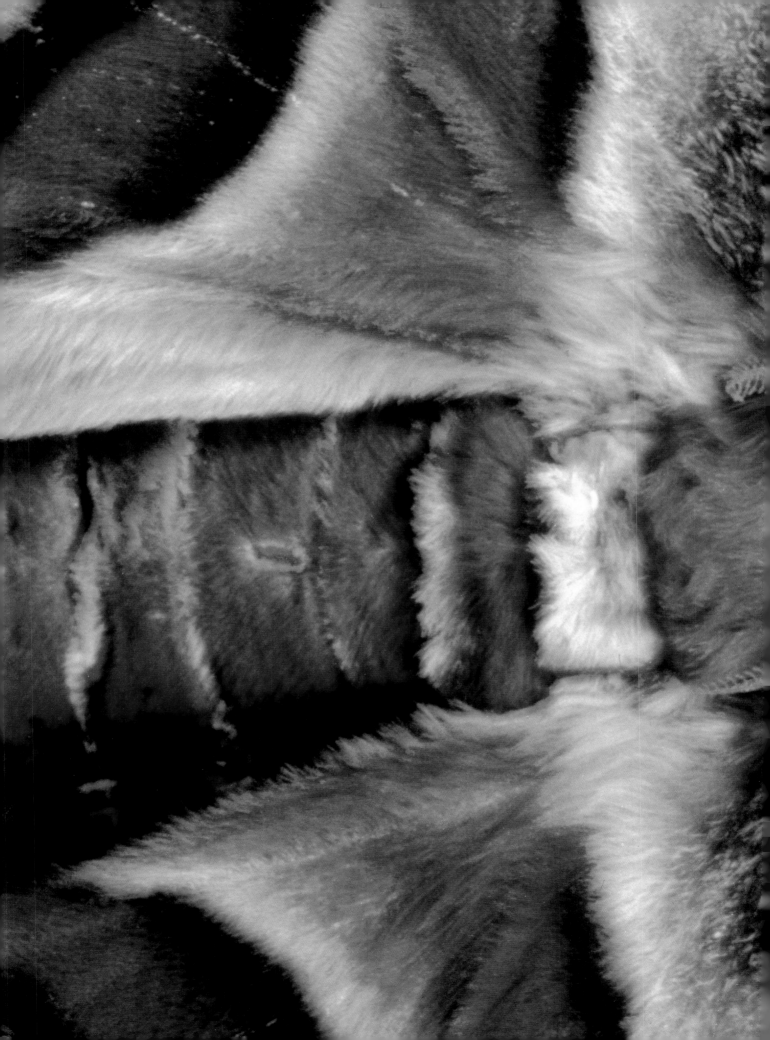

ATLAS MOTH

This female atlas moth is looking for a mate. She does not fly about searching but waits for a male to come to her. She sits on a leaf and releases a chemical substance called a pheromone to attract a male. If a predator tries to make a meal of her while she is waiting, the moth will quickly lift her wings. The tip of each wing looks just like a striking snake and will frighten away most attackers. After she mates, the moth starts to lay her eggs. She spends the whole night gluing the eggs to leaves and twigs.

From the time it begins life as an egg, the leaf insect is a master of disguise.

Warm, wet jungles are home to the leaf insect. It comes out at night to feed on the leaves of the guava tree and other trees.

HIDDEN EGGS

Up in the trees, the female leaf insect lays about 100 eggs, flicking them from her so that they fall to the forest floor below. The floor is covered with the droppings of the silk moth caterpillar. Because the eggs look just like these droppings, it's hard to tell them apart. This is the eggs' clever disguise to fool predators, such as birds and monkeys.

IMITATION ANTS

The eggs lie on the ground for about six months and then hatch. The skinny babies are 0.39 inch (1cm) long and bright red, just like the ants in the jungle—another trick on predators.

LEAF SHAPES

As the young grow, they turn green or brown and develop flaps of skin on both sides of their bodies that look just like the leaves of the trees around them.

SHORT LIVES

Leaf insects mate when the male is about 15 weeks old and the female is about 18 weeks old. The male dies a week or so later, but the female lives on for another six weeks after laying her eggs.

LEAF INSECT

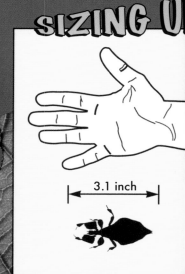

SIZING U[...]

3.1 inch

BEASTLY FACTS

- **SCIENTIFIC NAM[...]**
  Phyllium giganti[...]
- **SIZE:** Female up [...] to 5.9 inches lo[...] male up to 3.1 inch long
- **LIVES:** Malaysia[...]
- **EATS:** Leaves

ORCHID MANTIS

It may look like a harmless flower, but the orchid mantis is really a deadly killer.

Compared to human beings, mantises are very old. They have been on Earth for about 30 million years longer than people have! The orchid mantis lives in forests where flowers called orchids grow.

FLOWER POWER
With wide petal-like flaps on its legs and amazing coloring, this mantis looks just like one of the orchids in which it hides.

ORCHID MANTIS

PERFECT DISGUISE

Looking like a flower gives the orchid mantis the perfect disguise. Predators, such as birds and lizards, think it is just another orchid and leave it alone. This cunning disguise also helps it catch its prey.

DEADLY TRICK

Keeping very still, the mantis waits for a victim to come along. The only movement it makes is to rock gently backward and forward—just like a delicate flower swaying in the breeze. Unaware of this deadly trick, insects land on the orchids nearby to feed on the sweet nectar inside. When an insect is close enough, the mantis makes its move. It shoots out its front legs and grabs the victim, spiking it with its claws and the sharp spines on its legs so that the victim can't escape.

WATCH OUT!

Hoping to pick up some nectar, a bee buzzes toward an orchid. It aims for what it thinks is the center of a flower—and flies straight into the arms of a deadly orchid mantis.

Antennae sen victims as the past.

Large eyes spot even th slightest movement.

A flexible neck means that the mantis can easily spin its head around.

Sharp spines help trap struggling prey.

SIZING UP

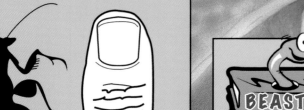

1.6–1.9 inch

BEASTLY FACTS

- **SCIENTIFIC NAME:** *Hymenopus coronatus*
- **SIZE:** 1.6–1.9 inch
- **LIVES:** Malaysia and other parts of Southeast Asia
- **EATS:** Other minibeasts such as grasshoppers, flies, moths, butterflies, and bees

Small Talk

BENDY NECK

The orchid mantis does not chase after its prey, so it has had to develop other ways of picking out possible victims. With its huge round eyes that stick out from the sides of its head, the mantis can see in every direction. It doesn't even need to turn around—this creature's neck is so bendy that it can spin its head right around to watch its victim approaching from behind!

LEFTOVERS

The mantis eats its prey alive. With its sharp jaws, it bites out pieces of flesh and chews them up until they are small enough to swallow. This meat eater has a good appetite and eats up all the soft, juicy parts of its victim. It is, however, quite fussy and will leave behind all the tough bits, such as the legs and wings. When the orchid mantis has finished, it carefully cleans the spines on each leg to make them ready for the next victim.

MALE AND FEMALE

The male and female orchid mantises look slightly different. The female is twice as big as her mate. Her size makes her a weak flier. Her wings are a pale color, while the male, a good flier, has transparent wings.

MOTHER AND BABIES

Orchid mantis eggs develop inside their mother's body. They are laid in a kind of foam, and three to six months later, the young hatch. They are bright red and pretend to be stinging ants to put predators off. As they grow and change into adults, they molt (shed their old skins) several times.

AT PRAYER

The orchid mantis belongs in the group of praying mantises. These minibeasts get their name because they sit very still and hold up their front legs in front of their faces, as if they are saying their prayers.

WOOD LOUSE
As night falls, the wood louse, also called a pill bug, crawls out where it is hidden from under a smelly piece of bark and stretches its jointed legs. It has been asleep all day and is now waking up—and it's hungry. It sets off on a nighttime scavenging trip, hoping to find some tasty food. Perhaps it will discover its favorite food—rotting leaves. The wood louse is a tough bug in its coat of armor. But it doesn't have any weapons to defend itself. If it gets into trouble, this minibeast curls up into a small, hard-to-spot ball and waits for danger to pass.

Small Talk

MULTITALENTED
Bugs mimic not just animals but a whole range of other things, including plants and rocks. There are even spiders and beetles that do very convincing impressions of bird droppings!

LOOK-ALIKE

Many bugs mimic other bugs and animals, either to protect themselves or to fool other bugs into coming close enough to be eaten.

Spectacled owl

An animal or plant can benefit from looking or acting like another animal or plant. This is called mimicry. One of the most common examples is when a type of bug protects itself against predators by mimicking another type of bug that is poisonous or has a painful bite or sting. Other examples are bugs that look and act like birds or leaves. Meet the masters of disguise.

THE OWL BUTTERFLY
The owl butterfly normally relies on its resemblance to a leaf to keep it out of harm's way. If it is disturbed, however, it has a trick up its sleeve. It suddenly opens its wings to reveal two huge eyespots. At the same time, it sticks out its body. To any predator the dead leaf has turned into an owl—one of the most feared enemies of small animals.

PEANUT HEAD MOTH
Like the owl butterfly, the peanut head moth uses its wings to do a good imitation of owl eyes. If you come at it from the front, however, you are in for a surprise. For there staring back at you is an alligator! It is true that it is only an inch or so long, but with staring eyes, flaring nostrils, and two rows of gleaming teeth, it would take a brave animal to start a fight with this cunning bug.

This bird (left) has had the shock of its life. A harmless butterfly, the owl butterfly, has opened its wings to reveal its eyespots, which look like the eyes of a clawed hunter—an owl. The real bird doesn't wait to take a second look; it flies off to safety.

LOOK A-LIKE

The harmless viceroy butterfly (below) has the same warning colors as the poisonous monarch butterfly (right).

Monarch butterfly

Wasps

Viceroy butterfly

The hoverfly (below) looks and flies just like a wasp (above). Unlike its look-alike, the hoverfly eats only nectar and doesn't sting.

THE ANT-MIMICKING FLY

The stlit-legged fly is unable to defend itself. Like a lot of stilt flies, it does not have a bite or sting. To try to scare off attackers it imitates a bug that can bite—an ant.

FIREFLIES

Fireflies use light to attract a mate. Each species has a special code of light flashes. The North American firefly uses its light for another purpose. By imitating the light flashes of another species of firefly, the female can lure an unsuspecting male to her. While the male is busy impressing the female, she lunges at him and eats him!

STINKBUGS

When baby stinkbugs are born they group together, face inward, and waggle their legs and antennae in the air. Together, they do an impressive impersonation of a caterpillar with irritating hairs on its body. Even a hungry bird won't be tempted.

Hoverfly

The harmless stilt-legged fly (below) tries to look dangerous. It folds its very small wings flat against its body so that it will be mistaken for a fierce ant (right).

Stilt-legged fly

Hawk moth caterpillar

Green vine snake

These two animals look similar, but they are not even distant relatives. This cunning hawk moth caterpillar (above left), which lives in Costa Rica, South America, does a brilliant impression of a snake (above right).

Is it true...

that some bugs imitate different things as they get older?

Yes. There is one bug, for example, called Macleay's spectre stick insect, that mimics four different things at different stages of its life. A master of mimicry, it can look like a seed when it's in the egg stage, a vicious ant when it hatches, a scorpion when it's young, and, finally, a dead leaf when it reaches adulthood.

Yellow desert scorpion

Macleay's spectre stick insect

Macleay's spectre stick insect (above) is constantly changing its image. Here, the young insect is doing its scorpion imitation.

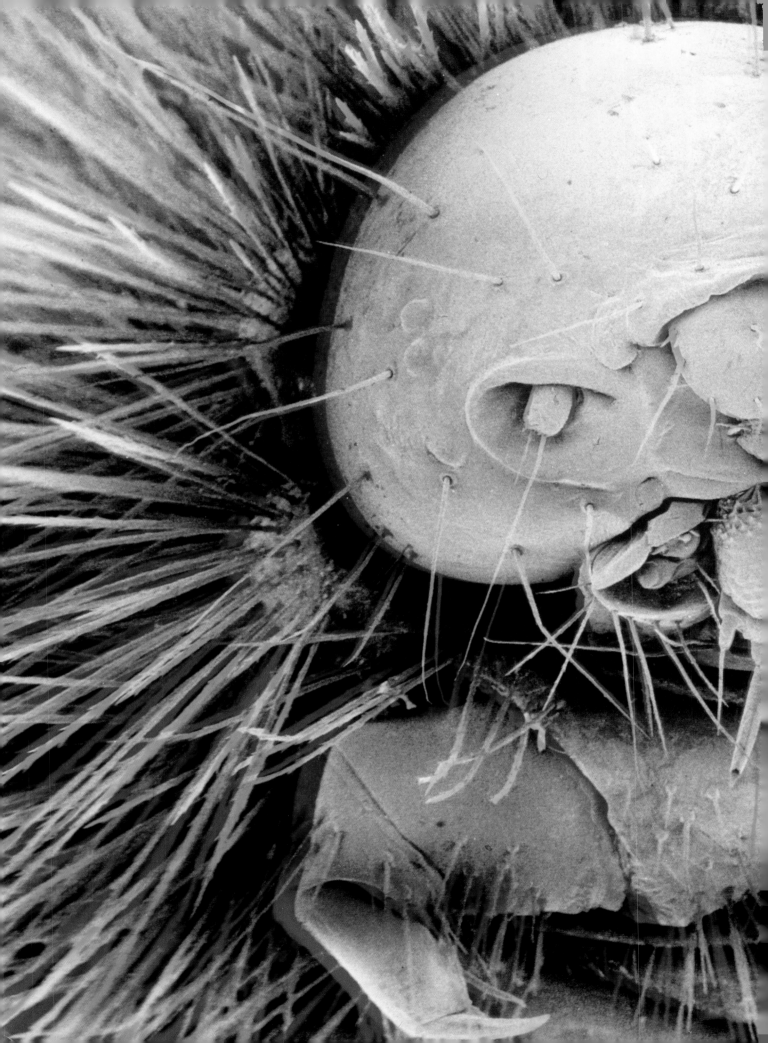

GARDEN TIGER LARVA

This orange and black caterpillar (larva) has just woken up from a long winter sleep. After hiding for six months, this hairy bug could eat a horse—or a few vegetable shoots. Suddenly, a gardener pushes a clump of green shoots to one side and pulls some carrots from the ground. Luckily, the human doesn't see the bug and simply carries on with his work. But the larva still isn't safe. A bird swoops down and is about to grab the larva in its beak when it spots the bug's warning colors and flies off. This caterpillar's hairs are designed to make it hard to swallow. The bird made a wise decision!